SIGHT-READ ANY RHYTHM INSTANTLY

INSTANTLY

BY MARK PHILLIPS

Also available:

Sight-Sing Any Melody Instantly, by Mark Phillips
(02500456)

ISBN 978-1-57560-515-9

Visit our website at www.cherrylane.com

PREFACE

About This Book

Have you ever looked at a complicated rhythmic figure and had no idea how to play it? If so, then this book is for you. You're not alone. Many students are unable to sight-read all but the simplest rhythms. Why is this? At the earliest stages of training, students are introduced to the relative time values of notes; they're taught how long each note lasts. "A half note gets this many beats, and a dotted eighth note gets that many beats," and so on. When students think in these terms, unless the rhythm is very simple, sight-reading problems invariably arise. Why? Because it's almost impossible to play correctly a series of notes whose time values involve complex fractions (a third of a beat, a quarter of beat, etc.).

The only way to sight-read rhythms fluently is to think not in terms of how long individual notes last, but in terms of what sound (or combination of sounds) might occur within each beat. This book shows you how to memorize the sound of each of the combinations of notes that commonly occur within *one beat*. If you think in terms of *beats*, you can sight-read successfully because the beat remains constant, and the rhythmic sound of each one-beat combination, having been previously memorized, can be played automatically.

What I Assume About You

I assume that you play an instrument or are just starting out on one; consequently, you probably have at least a rudimentary understanding of the basics of rhythmic notation. (But even if you don't, everything you need to know to understand the notation in this book is explained step-by-step as it occurs.) You should know the meanings of the terms *bar line, measure, time signature,* and *meter.* If you don't, check out their definitions at the back of the book in "Appendix A: Glossary." And you should also know the relative values of notes (for example, that a half note is equivalent to two quarter notes). But if you don't, see "Appendix B: The Relative Values of Notes."

Author's Note

Even though throughout this book you're asked to "tap" the rhythmic exercises, all of the examples may be performed in any convenient manner: tapping on a tabletop, clapping your hands, singing *la* or some other syllable, playing a repeated tone on an instrument, etc.

CONTENTS

CHAPTER 5: ALTERNATE NOTATIONS FOR FAMILIAR SOUNDS 35

CHAPTER 6: FURTHER COMPLICATIONS 44

Discussion: Counting Notes vs. Counting Beats

Before you tap any examples, let's talk about the difference between thinking in terms of *notes* and thinking in terms of *beats*. We'll take the 3/4 measure below as an example. (Note: If you don't understand what *3/4* or *measure* means, check out "Appendix A: Glossary" right now).

Here's how to think in terms of notes (the *wrong* way to think): You see that the measure above begins with a half note (which you know lasts for two beats), so you play it and count to two ("one-two"). Then, you see a quarter note (which you know lasts for one beat), so you play it and count to one ("one.") So altogether, you've counted "one-two, one."

Now let's see how to think in terms of beats (the *right* way to think): You use your knowledge of how long the notes last *only to identify where each of the beats begins and ends.* Now, here's the important part: For each beat in this measure you should determine only one thing—*whether or not you hit a note.* As you play the measure in question, in the back of your mind (half-consciously) you should say "one-two-three" (representing the three beats of the measure). But in the *front* of your mind you should say (consciously) "hit, don't hit, hit." This concept is so important that I'll say it again. *As you come to each beat of the measure, simply decide whether or not you hit a note.* That's really the whole trick. Now let's take the measure above beat by beat to see this in action:

Beat 1: You hit a note (because a note is indicated there).
Beat 2: You don't hit a note (because the half note you hit on beat 1 is still ringing).
Beat 3: You hit a note (because one is indicated there).

To summarize: *Don't* count "one-two, one." Instead, play (beat by beat): "hit, don't hit, hit" (or, to say it another way, "tap, nothing, tap").

Exercises:

A. Counting Beats in 2/4 Time

You'll notice that each beat in Exs. A-1 and A-2 (which are in 2/4 time) has been numbered. If it helps you to do so, place an "X" at each beat in which there'll be an *attack* (hit, tap). This way you can see at a glance which beats you'll hit and which you won't (the first few measures of Ex. A-1 have been started for you). If necessary, you can employ this visual aid on all of the examples in this chapter.

Now you're ready to begin tapping! Remember: In 2/4 time, the *quarter note* (♩) receives one beat and the *half note* (♩) two beats. Tap in a moderate tempo.

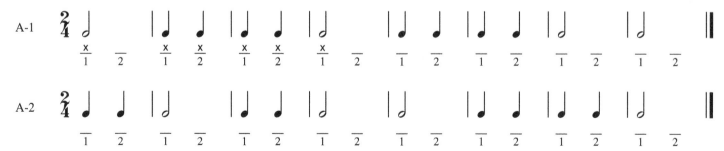

B. Counting Beats in 3/4 Time

In 3/4 time (and in other time signatures whose bottom number is "4"), the *dotted half note* (𝅗𝅥.) receives three beats. Remember: Don't count *notes*, count *beats* (and for each, decide whether you "hit" or "don't hit").

C. Counting Beats in 4/4 Time

In 4/4 time, the *whole note* (𝅝) receives four beats. Remember to count beats; for example, in measure 4 of Ex. C-1, don't count the whole note as "one-two-three-four." Instead, count those numbers half-consciously while you consciously think "hit, don't hit, don't hit, don't hit" (or "tap, nothing, nothing, nothing").

4/4 time may also be indicated by the symbol **c**, which stands for common time.

Discussion: Meter and Accentuation

Before going on to Exercise D, let's talk a little more about *meter* (the pattern of strong and weak beats dictated by the time signature). When you listen to music, you often feel beats in groups of two, three, or four. But how can you identify those particular groupings when you're listening to, say, a steady stream of quarter notes? Where does one grouping end and the next begin?

The performer can (and should) make you aware of these groupings of beats by the way he plays. How? Does he play the first note of each measure louder than the other notes? Well, he doesn't, but what he actually does is something like that: He *feels* the first beat of each measure as a *strong beat*. What's a strong beat? It's a beat that's given a mental emphasis in the mind of the performer, an emphasis that can be perceived by the listener.

Each meter has its own set pattern of strong and weak beats, and this pattern is an underlying framework that exists throughout a composition. But here's the important thing: The accentuation of the actual *notes* does not have to coincide with the mental accentuation of *beats*! A composer might choose, for instance, to indicate silences on the strong beats and very loud notes on the weak beats because he knows that the conflict between the *mental accentuation of beats* and the *actual accentuation of notes* can create rhythmic intensity.

In the examples you've tapped so far, you probably automatically gave a mental emphasis to the first beat of each measure. In 3/4 time, for example, you probably counted: ONE-two-three, ONE-two-three. If we use the symbol > to indicate a strong beat and the symbol – to indicate a weak beat, then here's how our metrical patterns look:

Some meters contain more than one strong beat per measure. When this happens, beat 1 is still given more mental emphasis than the other strong beat(s). We'll use the symbol (>) to indicate a beat that's strong, but not as strong as beat 1. Here's our metrical pattern for 4/4 time:

Why do you need to know all this if you're already emphasizing the right beats automatically? First, you need to be aware of the difference between an *accented note* (it's played louder and it might occur anywhere) and a *strong beat* (which is given only a mental emphasis and occurs regularly). Second, not all meters are so simple that you'll automatically emphasize the right beats. By using the symbols >, (>), and –, we'll be able to identify the strong and weak beats in the more complicated meters you'll be tapping later on.

Exercises:

D. The Quarter Rest

A silence that corresponds in duration to a quarter note is called a *quarter rest* (𝄽). Naturally, there should be no attack on any beat containing a rest.

We now have two situations in which there should be "no attack" on a given beat.

Situation 1: A note on a previous beat is sustained. (There's no attack on beat 2 of measure 4 of Ex. D-l, for example.)

Situation 2: A rest is indicated. (There's no attack on beat 2 of measure 1 of Ex. D-l, for example.)

The important thing here is that, in spite of a difference in performance—the difference between a continuation of a previous sound on the one hand, and a silence on the other—your thought process (the process of counting beats and determining, for each beat, whether or not there'll be an attack) should remain the same.

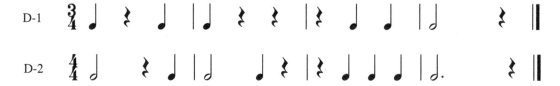

E. The Half Rest

A silence that corresponds in duration to a half note is called a *half rest* (⁻).

F. The Whole Rest

Unlike other rests, the *whole rest* (⁻) does not necessarily correspond in duration to a particular note value. The whole rest indicates a silence that lasts for an entire measure (in all meters).

G. The Tie

A *tie* (‿ or ⌒) is a curved line that joins together two notes of the same pitch. Its purpose is to indicate that there's no attack on the second note. The sound of the first note continues, uninterrupted, for the duration of the two notes.

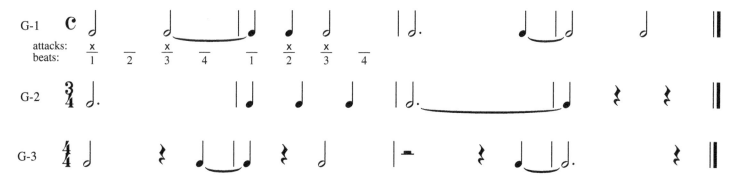

CHAPTER 2:
DIVIDING THE BEAT INTO TWO EQUAL PARTS

Discussion: The Sound of Two Attacks in One Beat

An *eighth note* (♪) is equal in duration to half a quarter note. Therefore, in time signatures whose bottom number is "4" (2/4, 3/4, and 4/4, for example), two eighth notes (♫) take up one beat.

You now need to memorize the sound of two eighth notes occurring in one beat. But what is that sound? Take a look at the example below.

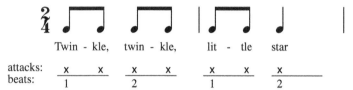

When you say the words "twinkle" and "little" in this song, you're pronouncing *two syllables in one beat*. What you're actually doing is performing eighth notes orally.

Now perform this (it might help to think of the words "twinkle, twinkle, twinkle," etc., with each word getting a beat):

Perform this (it might help to think of the words "star, twinkle, star, twinkle," etc., with each word getting a beat):

Perform this (it might help to think of the words "twinkle, star, twinkle, star," etc., with each word getting a beat):

Now that you've memorized the sound of two eighth notes occurring in one beat, you should have no trouble performing the examples below. The correct thought process is a simple one: *Count beats*. Whenever you see a beat containing two eighth notes, simply tap the sound you've memorized.

Discussion: Don't Say "And"

Here's something extremely important to remember. When you're playing rhythms involving eighth notes—as in Ex. A-1 (below), for instance—count *only* the beats ("one-two-three-four"). In spite of what anyone else may have told you or what you may have read in other books, never say *and* (that is, don't count "one-*and*, two-*and*, three-*and*, four-*and*"). Why? Because you need to keep the steadily flowing beat numbers in your *semiconscious* mind while the sound of previously memorized combinations of notes that can occur in each beat are up front in your *conscious* mind. If you say *and*, or—even worse—if, for playing sixteenth notes, you say the popular phrase *one-ee-and-uh*, you can't help but bring the underlying beat from your semiconscious into your conscious mind—and if you do that, those extra syllables, instead of helping matters, will only interfere (or even clash) with the execution of your various (previously memorized) one-beat note combinations.

Exercises:
A. Playing Two Eighths
Tap the following:

A-1

Four eighth notes are often beamed together.

Discussion: The Sound of the "Upbeat"

A silence that corresponds in duration to an eighth note is called an *eighth rest* (𝄾).

Up till now, we've dealt with three different sounds that might occur in one beat. (By the way, we're still dealing with time signatures whose bottom number is "4.")

First sound: An attack on the beat (♩)

Second sound: No attack (𝄽)

Third sound: Two attacks in one beat (♫)

Let's use the eighth rest to indicate a fourth sound: no attack on the "downbeat," which is the first half of the beat; then an attack on the "upbeat," which is the second half of the beat (𝄾 ♪).

You need to memorize this fourth sound. Imagine you're about to play two eighth notes, but then you substitute a silence for the first of the two notes; you play only the second note. Picture it like this: 𝄾♩ .

Perform this:

Now read the standard notation and perform the same thing:

Discussion: Naming All Four Sounds

Let's give a name to each of our four sounds.

1. Our first sound, an attack on the downbeat (♩), will be denoted by the letter "D," for "downbeat." A variation of this sound (♪ 𝄾) is performed differently (the note isn't sustained as long), but is still an attack on the downbeat and will also be denoted by the letter "D."

2. Our second sound, an attack on neither the downbeat nor the upbeat (𝄽 or a continuation of a previously attacked note, such as the second beat of ⅔ ♩) will be denoted by the letter "N," for "neither."

3. Our third sound, attacks on both the downbeat and the upbeat (♫) will be denoted by the letter "B," for "both."

4. Our fourth sound, an attack on the upbeat only (𝄾 ♪) will be denoted by the letter "U," for "upbeat." A variation of this sound (‿♫) is performed differently (the downbeat is a continuation of a previously attacked note), but is still an attack on the upbeat only and will also be denoted by the letter "U."

Exercises:

B. Playing All Four Sounds (Without Ties)

In Exs. B-1, B-2, and B-3, label each beat with the appropriate letter (D, N, B, or U).

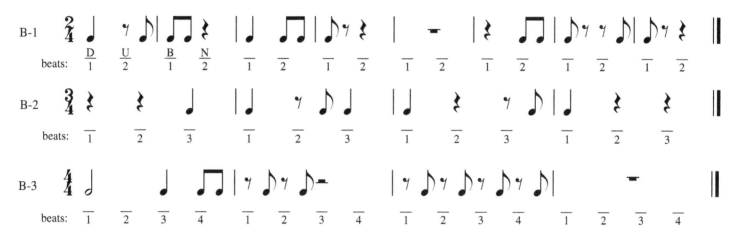

C. Playing All Four Sounds (With Ties)

Label each beat in Exs. C-1, C-2, and C-3.

Discussion: Visually Obscured Beats: Upbeat Quarter Notes

Up till now, all the examples have been notated in a way that shows clearly where each beat begins and ends. But notators often use alternate rhythmic notation for the sake of simplicity. For example, where we've been writing ♩ 𝅘𝅥𝅮𝅘𝅥𝅮 𝅘𝅥𝅮𝅘𝅥𝅮, another notator might have written ♩ ♪ ♩ ♪.

Why does the latter notation cause trouble for so many students? Because the beats have become visually obscured. It's no longer immediately apparent where one beat ends and the next begins.

Exercises:

D. Playing All Four Sounds (With Upbeat Quarter Notes)

In Exs. D-1 and D-2, draw a box around each beat. Next, label each beat with the letter D, N, B, or U. (Ex. D-1 has been started for you.) Now tap. Remember: A quarter note that begins on an upbeat is equivalent to two eighth notes tied together (♪♩ ♪ = 𝅘𝅥𝅮𝅘𝅥𝅮 𝅘𝅥𝅮𝅘𝅥𝅮).

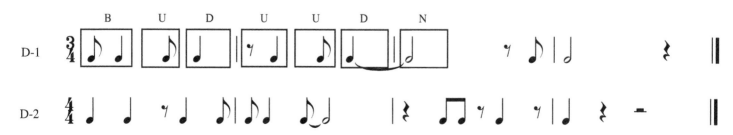

14

Discussion: Visually Obscured Beats: The Augmentation Dot

Another device notators use to simplify their written music is the *augmentation dot*. Where we've been writing
$\frac{2}{4}$ ♩♫, another notator might write $\frac{2}{4}$ ♩. ♪. And where we've been writing $\frac{2}{4}$ ♫♩, another notator might write
$\frac{2}{4}$ ♪♩.. That's because when a dot is placed next to a note, it adds to that note one half the note's value. Therefore,
a quarter note with a dot placed next to it is equivalent to a quarter note tied to an eighth note (or an eighth note
tied to a quarter note). Although in each of the above examples the latter notation is simpler in that it requires
fewer symbols, it doesn't show clearly where each beat begins and ends. That's why many students encounter
difficulty in reading dotted rhythms.

Exercises:

E. Playing All Four Sounds (With the Augmentation Dot)

If necessary, draw a box around each beat in Exs. E-1 and E-2, then label each beat with the letter D, N, B, or U.

F. Putting It All Together

Tap the following. Label each beat if necessary.

Watch for the meter changes in the next exercise. In the 3/4 bar, count only three beats.

Discussion: The Half Note Gets the Beat: 2/2 "Cut" Time

Up till now, we've been dealing with time signatures whose bottom number is 4. That bottom number told us that the quarter note received the beat. Therefore, the sound we labeled "D" was indicated by a quarter note; the sound we labeled "N" was indicated by a quarter rest; the sound we labeled "B" was indicated by two eighth notes; and the sound we labeled "U" was indicated by an eighth rest followed by an eighth note.

In 2/2 time, the bottom number "2" tells us that the *half note* is to receive one beat. Therefore, our four memorized sounds look like this in 2/2 time:

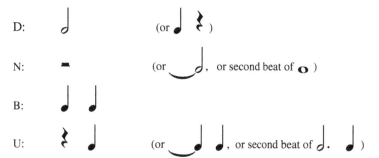

Of course, the top number of the 2/2 signature tells us that each measure will contain two beats.

2/2 time is usually indicated by the symbol ₵, and is usually referred to as "cut time" or "alla breve."

Some students have the mistaken idea that cut time means to play at double speed. But the speed, or tempo, of a composition is determined not by the time signature, but by the tempo heading or metronome indication. And here's the important thing: The tempo indication refers to the speed of the *beats,* not the notes.

Yet this misconception persists. Why? Let's compare three examples.

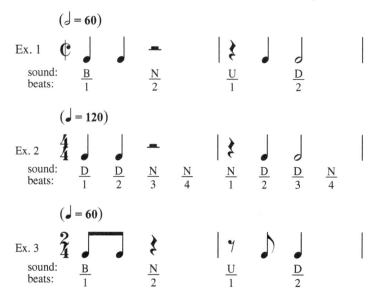

16

The delusion persists because students realize that, tempos being equal, a quarter note in cut-time is indeed played twice as fast as a quarter note in 4/4 time. But by simply doubling the speed of the notes, they end up playing Ex. 2 when they're trying to play Ex. 1! You can see how different these two examples are. Ex. 1 contains four slow beats. Ex. 2 contains eight fast beats. The feeling is entirely different.

What's important to realize is that Ex. 1 is actually equivalent to Ex. 3. Each measure contains two slow beats.

Remember this: Never think of cut time as being twice as fast as 4/4, since there's no reason to compare the two signatures in the first place. Only the tempo indication tells you the speed of the beats, and only the time signature tells you which note receives the beat. Cut time is merely 2/2 time—no more, no less; it's two beats per measure with the half note receiving the beat.

Exercises:

G. Playing in 2/2 and 3/2 Time

In the next example, draw a box around each beat, then label each beat with the letter D, N, B, or U.

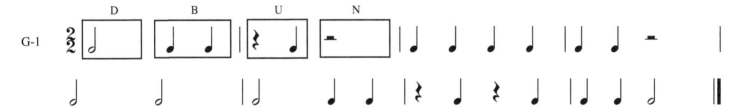

In the following examples, label each beat if necessary.

In 3/2 time, each measure contains three beats, with the half note receiving the beat. (Since the half note receives one beat, the whole note receives two beats, and the dotted whole note, being equivalent to a whole note tied to a half note, receives three beats.)

Watch for the changing meters.

CHAPTER 3:
DIVIDING THE BEAT INTO THREE EQUAL PARTS

Discussion: 6/8 Time (9/8 and 12/8, Too)

In a song like "Twinkle, Twinkle, Little Star," each beat naturally divides itself into two equal parts. In this chapter, you'll tap rhythms in which the beat naturally divides itself into *three* equal parts.

But how do we notate three equal notes that take up one beat? How do we notate this famous rhythm, for example?

```
        Fol-low the yel-low brick  |  road
beats: 1              2            |  1      2
```

Knowing that we want two beats in each measure, we might consider using a 2/4 time signature. The problem is that in 2/4 time, there *is* no single note value that takes up a third of a beat. This rules out the possibility of allowing the quarter note to receive the beat. To receive the beat we need a note value that's divisible by three. One choice is the dotted quarter note (♩.), which can be divided into three equal eighth notes.

Then what's our time signature to be when we notate "Follow the Yellow Brick Road"? The top number should be "2," because we want two beats in each measure. The bottom of the time signature should tell us that the dotted quarter note receives the beat. We need a signature that looks like this:

(Two beats per bar)→ **2**
(Dotted quarter note receives the beat)→ ♩.

But here we run into further complications because we need a numeral—not a note—to serve as the bottom half of the time signature. But there *is* no numeral that can tell us that the dotted quarter note receives the beat. Apparently, we are stuck. Yet, notators have surmounted this obstacle by writing the misleading 6/8 instead of the non-existing 2/♩..

Why do I say 6/8 is misleading? Because 6/8 implies that each measure contains six beats, with the eighth note receiving the beat. But surely, when we sing:

we are singing only *two* beats, with the *dotted quarter note* receiving the beat.

But notators have chosen 6/8 for this type of music because it's the closest they can get to 2/♩.. (And at least it adds up!) What you have to keep in mind is that when you see a 6/8 signature, it's probably telling you to play in 2/♩..

Here's yet another complication. How do we notate music that actually *does* contain six beats per measure with the eighth note receiving the beat? Wouldn't this also be notated in 6/8 time? If so, when we see 6/8, how do we know whether to play six or two beats per measure?

The 6/8 signature indeed has a dual function. It can imply either six or two beats per measure. How do we tell one 6/8 from the other? The tempo heading should guide you. You'll know that 2/♩. is intended when the phrase "in 2" appears as part of the heading, as in "Moderately, in 2." You'll also know that 2/♩. is intended when a metronome indication is given that tells you to play so many dotted quarter notes per minute, as in ♩. = 88.

On the contrary, you'll know that a true 6/8 (six beats per measure) is intended when the tempo heading includes the phrase "in 6," or when the metronome indication tells you to play so many eighth notes per measure. But even in true 6/8, the 1st and 4th beats are stressed (just as the 1st and 4th eighth notes in two-beat 6/8 are stressed).

What if the tempo heading doesn't guide with either of these directions? What if the tempo heading simply says "Moderately"? In that case, the tempo heading isn't telling you everything you need to know (and that's the fault of the notator). But you can use this as a rule of thumb: In moderate or fast tempos, assume 6/8 means 2/♩.; in slow tempos, 6/8 may very well mean "true" 6/8.

For the time being, let's forget about "true" 6/8. In this chapter we'll concentrate on the more frequently used, two-beat 6/8, because, after all, our goal here is to divide one beat into three equal parts.

But now let's go a step further. Consider the following: In a measure that contains two dotted quarter note beats (♩. ♩.), we have a total of six eighth notes (♫♪ ♫♪), and our time signature is 6/8. In a measure that contains *three* dotted quarter note beats (♩. ♩. ♩.), we have total of *nine* eighth notes (♫♪ ♫♪ ♫♪), so our time signature is 9/8. (Just as 6/8 really means 2/♩., 9/8 really means 3/♩. . And when we have *four* dotted quarter note beats in a measure (♩. ♩. ♩. ♩.), we have a total of *twelve* eighth notes (♫♪ ♫♪ ♫♪ ♫♪), so our time signature is 12/8. (Of course, 12/8 really means 4/♩. .

Discussion: The Sound of Three Attacks in One Beat

Each different combination of notes that might occur in one beat is a different "sound." If the eighth note is our smallest unit, then in 6/8, 9/8, and 12/8 time we have eight basic sounds. We won't give them names, but you should memorize each one. The first two you've already memorized.

Sound 1: ♩. (an attack on the downbeat)

Sound 2: 𝄽., or _♩., or beat 2 of ♩., or any beat of ▬ (no attack). Note: A dot placed after a rest serves the same function as a dot placed after a note—it increases its value by one half.

Sound 3: ♫♪ (three equal attacks in one beat) This sound can be learned by saying:

"Fol - low   the   yel - low   brick"

Exercises:

A. Playing Three Eighths in One Beat
Tap the following:

Here are two variations of Sound 1: (𝅘𝅥𝅭)

Variation 1: 𝅘𝅥 𝄿

Variation 2: 𝅘𝅥𝅮 𝄿 𝄿

Each of these variations is an attack on the downbeat only, but in each the note isn't sustained for the entire beat.

Discussion: Learning the Sounds of Various Combinations of Notes

How do you learn the sound of a particular combination of notes that occurs in one beat if there doesn't happen to be a convenient famous song that perfectly demonstrates the sound?

The answer may sound contradictory to everything I've said up till now; nevertheless, here it is: You subdivide the beat mathematically. Why do I say this after having told you not to subdivide the beat? In performance (which can include sight-reading) you should never subdivide the beat. You don't need to—the sound of each one-beat note combination has been previously memorized. But in first learning the sound of a particular combination of notes that occur in one beat so that you can memorize it, what choice do you have but to subdivide the beat? The "famous song" method can't work for every possible combination of notes.

How does subdividing the beat help teach you the sound of a particular combination of notes? Like this: In 6/8 time, for example, you realize that each beat is made up of three eighth notes, so in each beat you feel a fast "one-two-three." By looking at the notes in question, you can determine mathematically where in the beat each attack will occur. For example, when you see 𝅘𝅥𝅮𝄿𝅘𝅥𝅮, you know that there'll be attacks on the first and third eighth notes of the beat. How does this sound? Count to "three" quickly, and attack a note on "one" and "three." It may help to think of it like this:

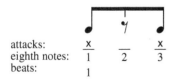

attacks:	x	_	x
eighth notes:	1	2	3
beats:	1		

There! You've played it, so now you've heard it. Play it again. Listen to the sound. Memorize it by playing the sound over and over, like this:

This, then, will be your procedure for learning the sound of a new combination of notes:

1. Determine mathematically where in the beat attacks will occur.
2. Play the notes and listen to the sound.
3. Memorize the sound.

Of course, you'll be sure to work out and memorize these sounds *before* performance. That way, when you sight-read, you won't have to think about anything but counting beats.

Exercises:

B. Attacking "One" and "Three"

In Exs. A-1 and A-2, you tapped three different sounds. In Exs. B-1 and B-2, in addition to tapping these sounds, you'll also tap two variations of the first sound mentioned above ♩ ♪ and ♪ ♪ ♪, a fourth sound ♫♩, and a variation of the fourth sound (♩ ♪). Learn and memorize these sounds before you tap the following examples.

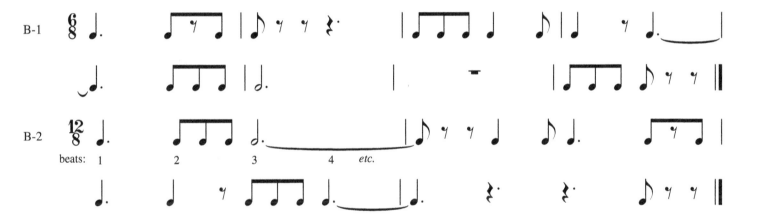

C. Attacking "Three"

Here's our fifth sound: ♪ ♪, and a variation of it ♩ ♪. Learn and memorize it, then tap the following:

Tap one beat per measure in the following example. Think of 3/8 as 1/♩. .

D. Attacking "Two" and "Three"

Our sixth sound is ♪ ♫; a variation of it is ♪♫♩. Don't forget to learn and memorize it before you tap.

E. Attacking "One" and "Two"

Here's our seventh sound: ♫ ♪; a variation of it is ♩ ♪.

F. Attacking "Two"

Our eighth sound is ♪ ♪ ♪. Three variations are ♪ ♩, ♫ ♪, and ♪ ♩.

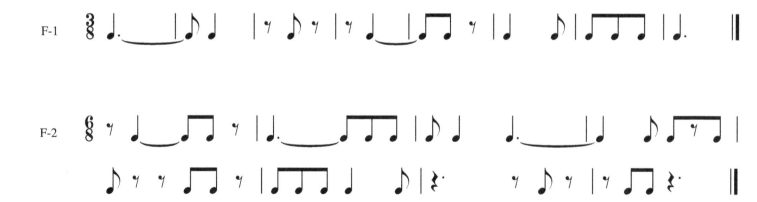

Discussion: Compound and Simple Meter; Duple and Triple Meter; 6/4 Time vs. 3/2 Time

In Chapter 2 you tapped rhythms in which the beat naturally divided itself into two equal parts. At first we allowed the quarter note to receive the beat. Later, we allowed the half note to receive the beat. Theoretically, we could have allowed other note values to receive the beat, such as the eighth note, in which case we would have seen time signatures such as 4/8 and 8/8; or the whole note, in which case we would have seen time signatures such as 2/1, 3/1, and 4/1. We didn't tap exercises in these meters, however, because notators use them so infrequently.

It may interest you to know that there's a term used to describe meters in which the beat naturally divides itself into two equal parts. That type of music is said to be in *simple* meter.

In this chapter you've been tapping rhythms in *compound* meter. In compound meter, the beat naturally divides itself into *three* equal parts. So far, we've used only the dotted quarter note to receive the beat. Theoretically, any dotted note can be used to receive the beat in compound meter (because any dotted note can be divided into three equal parts)—but, other than the dotted quarter note, only the dotted half note is used with any regularity in this way.

What time signature do we write if we want, say, one beat per measure with the dotted half note receiving the beat? We would like to use 1/𝅗𝅥.. But just as 1/♪. had to be written as 3/8, 1/𝅗𝅥. must be written as 3/4! How can 3/4 time suddenly be a compound meter when in Chapter 2 it was a simple meter? Just as there's a "true" 6/8 (six beats per measure) and a two-beat 6/8 (really 2/♩.), there's a "true" 3/4 (three beats per measure with the beat naturally dividing itself into two equal parts) and a one-beat 3/4 (really 1/𝅗𝅥., with the beat naturally dividing itself into three equal parts). Again, the tempo heading helps you to know which 3/4 is which. When the heading contains the phrase "in 1" or a metronome indication tells you to play so many dotted half notes per minute, then 3/4 really means 1/𝅗𝅥., and the meter is compound. If the heading lacks these indications, a "true" 3/4 is intended, and the meter is simple. In the examples below, you can compare the two types of 3/4.

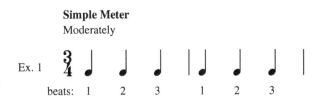

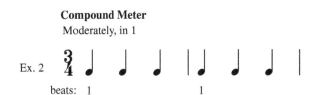

Let's go a step further. What if we want the dotted half note to receive the beat, but we want two beats per measure? Then we'd like to see the signature 2/𝅗𝅥.. But just as 1/𝅗𝅥. is written 3/4, 2/𝅗𝅥. is written 6/4.

6/4 time is a source of confusion for many students because they're not sure what the difference is between (1) 6/4 and 6/8, (2) two-beat 6/4 and six-beat 6/4, and (3) 6/4 and 3/2. Let's take these points one at a time.

(1) What's the difference between Exs. 3 and Ex. 4 below?

There's no difference in performance—the distinctions are purely visual. Each example contains two beats, with each beat naturally dividing itself into three equal parts. Because the quarter note in Ex. 3 is equal to the eighth note in Ex. 4, some students become confused—and why shouldn't they when they're so used to being told that a quarter note lasts twice as long as an eighth note? But of course, what they have been told so often is only *sometimes* true. What you need to keep in mind is that in the two examples above, as in all music, the tempo heading refers to the speed of the *beats,* not the notes. The choice of the individual notes that together make up one beat depends on the type of note that's to receive the beat, which, in turn, is dictated by the time signature.

But there's still another reason students become confused. In 6/4 writing, there's often a lack of beams which, if present, would make the beats immediately recognizable. In Ex. 3, for instance, students have no visual guide to tell them that beat 2 begins on the fourth quarter note. So, what you have to keep in mind when you read 6/4 time is that in each measure there are *two* groups of three quarter notes, like this ♩♩♩ ♩♩♩ , just as in 6/8 time there are two groups of three eighth notes (♫♪ ♫♪ |).

But why should music be written in 6/4 time when it could be written in 6/8 time instead? Why do we need two ways of writing the same thing? The notator (who is often the composer) chooses the time signature. He wants his notation to be easily read and understood. He often chooses 6/8 because he knows that eighth beams (♫♪ ♫♪) make the beats immediately recognizable. On the other hand, his music might contain many minute subdivisions of the beat. In 6/8 time, the numerous beams that would be required would made reading awkward and difficult. He chooses 6/4 time to cut the number of beams in half.

(2) What's the difference between Exs. 5 and Ex. 6 below?

There's very little visual difference, but there's a great difference in performance. And what is that difference? Before answering that question, we need to talk a little more about meter.

We've spoken of meters as being either *simple* (the beat naturally divides itself into two equal parts; an undotted note receives the beat) or *compound* (the beat naturally divides itself into three equal parts; a dotted note receives the beat). We can also speak of meters as being *duple, triple,* or *quadruple.* These terms refer to the number of beats in each measure. In duple meters, there are *two* beats in each measure (2/4, 2/2, and 6/8 are examples of duple meters). In triple meters, there are *three* beats in each measure (3/4, 3/2, and 9/8 are examples of triple meters). In quadruple meters, there are *four* beats in each measure (4/4 and 12/8 are examples of quadruple meters). What if there are more than four beats in a measure? Then we can speak of *quintuple* time (five beats), *sextuple* time (six beats), *septuple* time (seven beats), and so on.

Often we speak of meters in terms of how the beat is divided (into two equal parts or into three equal parts) *and* in terms of the number of beats in each measure (two, three, four, etc.). We say that 2/4 time, for example, is "simple duple." And you can see that it is:

Simple → natural division of beats into two equal parts:

Duple → two beats per measure:

We say that 9/8 time, for example, is "compound triple." And you can see that it is:

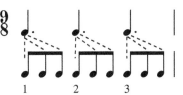

Compound → natural division of beats into three equal parts:

Triple → three beats per measure:

How can we refer to 3/4 time? That's right—it's *simple triple,* or three beats per measure with each beat dividing itself into two equal parts.

Now let's take another look at Exs. 5 and 6 and describe their meters. Ex. 5, having *two beats per measure* with each beat dividing itself into *three equal parts,* is in *compound duple* time. Ex. 6, having *six beats per measure* with each beat dividing itself into *two equal parts,* is in *simple sextuple* time.

In Exs. 5 and 6, it should now be apparent that there must be a difference in performance, because the meters are entirely different. Ex. 5 is played the same as this:

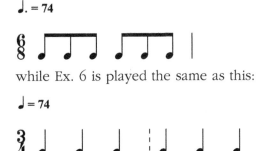

while Ex. 6 is played the same as this:

(3) Now that you understand how to describe meters, it should be easy for you to understand the differences between 3/2 and 6/4. Let's compare three examples:

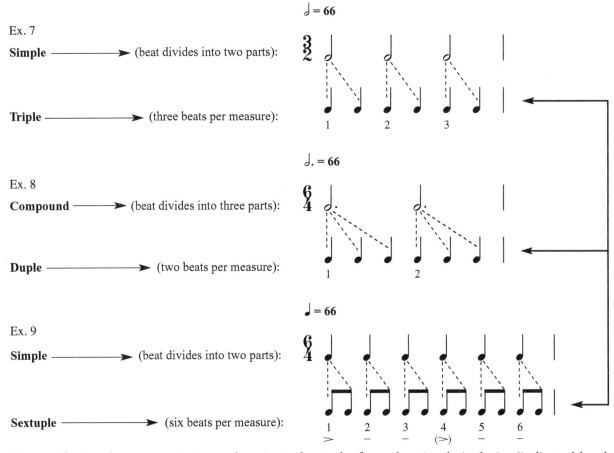

Ex. 7

Simple ⟶ (beat divides into two parts):

Triple ⟶ (three beats per measure):

Ex. 8

Compound ⟶ (beat divides into three parts):

Duple ⟶ (two beats per measure):

Ex. 9

Simple ⟶ (beat divides into two parts):

Sextuple ⟶ (six beats per measure):

Any confusion that may exist in students' minds results from the visual similarity (indicated by the arrows at the right above) among these three examples. How can you sight-read successfully in spite of these similarities? It all comes down to our basic premise: Think in terms of *beats,* not *notes.* Your awareness of meter allows you to identify beats. And in the three examples above, while the notes may be visually similar, the beats are not.

Exercises:

G. The Dotted Half Note Gets the Beat

Since this chapter is concerned with compound time, in the exercises below, tap 6/4 as compound duple, not simple sextuple. Likewise, tap 9/4 as compound triple, and 12/4 as compound quadruple. You'll be tapping the same eight sounds (and their variations) that you tapped in Exercises A–F of this chapter—but since the dotted *half* note is now receiving the beat, those sounds must be notated so that each beat is made up of three *quarter* notes, not three eighth notes.

CHAPTER 4:
DIVIDING THE BEAT INTO FOUR EQUAL PARTS

Discussion: Sixteenth Notes and the Sound of Four Attacks in One Beat

We can continue to divide the beat into smaller and smaller fractions. In Chapter 2 you divided the beat into two equal parts; in Chapter 3 into three equal parts. In this chapter you'll divide the beat into four equal parts. We could go on indefinitely! The question is, when should we stop? How many different sounds do you need to memorize before you can become a successful rhythmic sight-reader?

Fortunately, you don't need to memorize the sound of every possible combination of notes that might ever occur in one beat; that would be impossible. Instead, you need to memorize only the sounds of those combinations of notes that *often* occur in one beat. By having the sounds of those often-used combinations in your head, you can be a fluent rhythmic sight-reader.

But what about those irregular combinations of notes that you won't memorize? Won't they destroy your sight-reading performance? Remember: Sight-reading isn't meant to be a finished performance. No one expects perfection from a sight-reader. If it's your intention during sight-reading never to interrupt the rhythmic flow, never to slow down or stop, then you'll recognize one of these irregular combinations as one beat's worth of music, and you'll do the best you can with it during that one beat. Then, on the next beat, whose sound will probably be a familiar one, you'll still be in tempo. If, on the other hand, you're not concerned about stopping or slowing down, you can teach yourself the sound of an irregular combination of notes by working it out mathematically.

Now let's divide the beat into four equal parts. If we tap in a meter whose time signature has the bottom number "4," then the quarter note will receive the beat. To indicate four equal notes that take up the time of one quarter note beat, we write four sixteenth notes: ♬♬ (it works out mathematically: 4 x 1/16 = 1/4).

The sight-reading of sixteenth notes often causes tremendous difficulties for would-be sight-readers. Why is this? A sight-reader who thinks in terms of notes instead of beats has the unpleasant task of keeping track of the duration of many short notes, each of which might last for only a small fraction of a second—a mind-boggling feat! But you don't need to concern yourself with the exact duration of individual sixteenth notes; instead, you should *memorize* the sound of the various combinations of sixteenth notes that might occur in one beat. Then, you need keep track of only *beats*. You should automatically play the notes correctly, because the sound of each possible combination will have been memorized!

If the sixteenth note is our smallest unit, then in simple time there are sixteen different sounds that might occur in one beat. We'll take these sounds one at a time, and you'll learn and memorize each one. (These will be the last sounds you'll need to memorize to become a fluent rhythmic sight-reader.) How do you teach yourself the sound of a particular combination of sixteenth notes that take up one beat? Again, subdivide the beat mathematically. Realize that each beat is made up of a fast "one-two-three-four." Determine mathematically where in the beat attacks will occur. Play the sound over and over until it's memorized.

Exercises:

A. Playing Four Sixteenths in One Beat

Here's our first sound: ♬♬. It sounds kind of like the word *Copenhagen* (if you say the syllables evenly during the time of one beat). But let's look at these notes in the context of what you might call a fast "one-two-three-four."

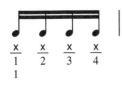

attacks:	x	x	x	x
sixteenth notes:	1	2	3	4
beats:	1			

The chart above helps you see where in the beat attacks occur. You might want to make a similar chart for all of the sounds presented in this chapter. But remember: Think of a fast "one-two-three-four" *only* when you're teaching yourself the sound of a new combination of notes. When you actually sight-read, think only of *beats!*

After you've memorized the sound of four equal attacks in one beat, tap the following:

B. Attacking "One," "Three," and "Four"

Here's our next sound ♩♫ . Where in the beat do attacks occur?

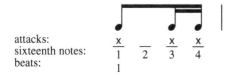

attacks:	x	—	x	x
sixteenth notes:	1	2	3	4
beats:	1			

The chart shows that attacks occur on the first, third, and fourth sixteenth notes. Learn and memorize this sound, then tap the following:

Here's a variation of the sound: ♪♫ (attacks still occur on the first, third, and fourth sixteenth notes, but the first note is shorter). Note: A rest that's equivalent to a sixteenth note is called a *sixteenth rest* (𝄿).

C. Attacking "One," "Two," and "Three"

Here's our next sound: ♫♩ . Where in the beat do attacks occur? Learn and memorize the sound.

In an effort to simplify notation, notators often write one larger note instead of two smaller tied notes. Compare and tap Exs. C-2 and C-3.

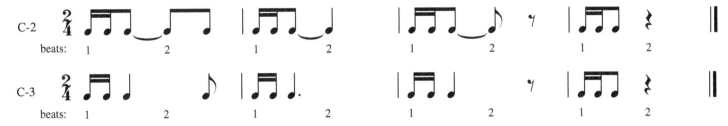

Here's a variation of the sound: ♫♪ ₇.

D. Attacking "One" and "Four"

Here's our next sound: ♪.♪ (a dotted eighth note is equivalent to an eighth note plus a sixteenth note, which is equivalent to three sixteenth notes).

Here are two variations of the sound: (1) ♪₇♪, (2) ♪₇♪ (or ♪₇₇♪).

E. Attacking "Four"

Here's our next sound: ₇·♪ (the dotted eighth rest is equivalent to an eighth rest plus a sixteenth rest).

Here are three variations of the sound: (1) ♪.♪, (2) ♪₇♪, (3) ♪₇♪.

F. Variations on Old Sounds

Our next four sounds are merely variations of the four basic sounds ("D", "N", "B", and "U") that you memorized in Chapter 2.

An attack on the downbeat only ("D") was notated in Chapter 2 like this: ♩; or like this: ♪ ₇. Here are two more variations: (1) ♪. ₇, (2) ♪₇.

An attack on neither the downbeat nor the upbeat ("N") was notated in Chapter 2 like this: 𝄽 (or this: ◡♩ or ◡♪ ₇). Here are two more variations: (1) ◡♪. ₇, (2) ◡♪₇.

An attack on both the upbeat and the downbeat ("B") was notated in Chapter 2 like this: ♫. Here are three variations: (1) ♫ ₇, (2) ♪₇♪, (3) ♪₇♪ ₇.

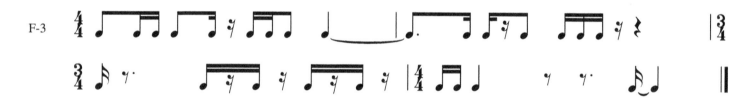

An attack on the upbeat only ("U") was notated in Chapter 2 like this: ₇ ♪; or this: ◡♫. Here are four more variations: (1) ₇ ♪₇, (2) ◡♫ ₇, (3) ◡♪₇♪, (4) ◡♪₇♪ ₇.

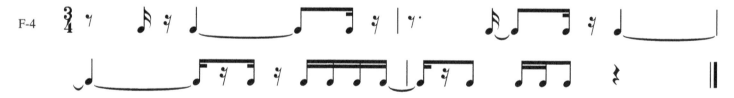

G. Attacking "One" and "Two"

Learn and memorize this sound: ♫. . Here are two variations: (1) ♫ ₇, (2) ♫ ₇.

H. Attacking "Three" and "Four"

Here's our next sound: ♪ 𝅘𝅥𝅮 . Here are two variations: (1) 𝅘𝅥𝅮𝅘𝅥𝅮, (2) 𝅘𝅥𝅮𝅘𝅥𝅮.

Again, notators often write one larger note instead of two smaller tied notes. Compare and tap Exs. H-2 and H-3.

I. Attacking "Two," "Three," and "Four"

Learn and memorize this sound: ♪ 𝅘𝅥𝅮𝅘𝅥𝅮 . Here's a variation: 𝅘𝅥𝅮𝅘𝅥𝅮𝅘𝅥𝅮 .

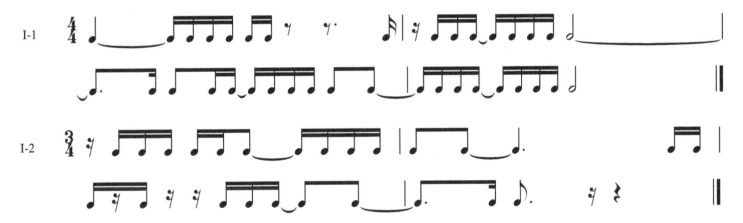

J. Attacking "One," "Two," and "Four"

Here's our next sound: 𝅘𝅥𝅮𝅘𝅥𝅮 . Here's a variation: 𝅘𝅥𝅮𝅘𝅥𝅮 .

K. Attacking "Two" and "Three"

Learn and memorize this sound: ♧ ♫. Here are three variations: (1) ♧ ♫ ♧, (2) ♫♫, (3) ♫♫ ♧.

L. Attacking "Two"

Here's our next sound: ♧ ♪. ; and two variations: (1) ♧ ♪ ♧, (2) ♧ ♪♧.

Here are three more variations: (1) ♫♩, (2) ♫♧, (3) ♫♧.

M. Attacking "Two" and "Four"

Here's our last sound: ♧ ♫; and three variations: (1) ♧♫♧, (2) ♫♫, (3) ♫♫♧.

This example contains all sixteen sounds.

Discussion: Dividing the Half Note Beat into Four Equal Parts

In all of the examples above, each quarter note beat consisted of four sixteenth notes (or their equivalent). But in 2/2 or 3/2 time, in which the *half* note receives the beat, each beat consists of four *eighth* notes (or their equivalent). In the examples below, you'll tap the same sixteen sounds you just learned, but they'll be notated differently because the half note will now be receiving the beat. For the purpose of illustration, let's visually compare the notation of some of these sounds when the quarter receives the beat and when the half note receives the beat.

One Quarter Note Beat   **One Half Note Beat**

Remember: In spite of visual differences, each rhythmic figure above is identical in sound to its partner on the opposite side of the chart.

Exercises:

N. The Half Note Gets the Beat

Tap the following:

CHAPTER 5:
ALTERNATE NOTATIONS FOR FAMILIAR SOUNDS

Discussion: Eighth Note Triplets

Each meter dictates a particular pattern of strong and weak beats, and each meter implies a natural subdivision of each beat into either two or three parts. In all of the examples in the previous chapters, there was a correlation between the *implied* subdivision of the beat (into two equal parts in simple time or three equal parts in compound time) and the *actual* subdivision of the beat into a particular combination of notes. For example, in simple time, in which the implied subdivision of the beat is into *two* equal parts, you tapped *two* eighth notes (or their equivalent) in each beat. Likewise, in compound time, in which the implied subdivision of the beat is into *three* equal parts, you tapped *three* eighth notes (or their equivalent) in each beat.

But in spite of any natural or implied subdivision of the beat, isn't a composer free to write whatever he chooses in each beat? Of course he is! Let's say, then, that a composer is writing in 2/4 time, and at some point in the composition he wishes to write three equal notes in one beat. How can he notate this when there exists no note that's equal to one third of a quarter note? Let's look at two possible solutions. The first solution, which is by far the less desirable, is to change meter for the measure(s) containing the irregular beat(s). Here's an example:

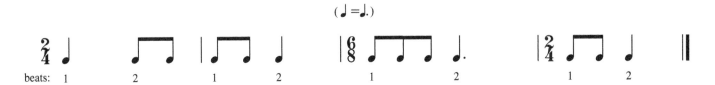

The equivalency (♩=♩.) placed above the 6/8 shows that the quarter note (one beat) in the 2/4 measure is equal to the dotted quarter note (one beat) in the 6/8 measure. Therefore, the 6/8 measure lasts exactly as long as the 2/4 measure (two beats).

If the change of meter solves our notational problem, why do I say that this solution is undesirable? There are two reasons. First, music that contains meter changes is more difficult to sight-read than music that's written in only one meter. Why? Because when you're confronted by a meter change, your sense of the underlying rhythmic framework (the pattern of strong and weak beats and the implied, natural subdivision of the beat) is momentarily lost—and your brain needs time to adjust to the new time signature.

The other reason the change-of-meter solution is undesirable is that, in the example above, the 6/8 notation is actually misleading (and therefore not entirely accurate). Why? Because in a 2/4 composition, there's an implied subdivision of the beat into two equal parts. So, in beat 1 of measure 3 of the above example, there *should be* a conflict between the implied subdivision of the beat (into two parts) and the actual subdivision of the beat (into three parts). This conflict would make the first beat of measure 3 sound like an oddity—something foreign to the underlying framework. But by writing measure 3 in 6/8 time, this all-important conflict is lost—because in 6/8 time the beat is *supposed* to divide itself into three equal parts!

Now let's look at the more desirable solution to our notational problem.

The figure that appears on beat 1 of measure 3 (♪♪♪) is called a *triplet* (in this case it's an *eighth note triplet* because it's made up of eighth notes). What's a triplet? It's a group of *three* equal notes (with the numeral "3" placed above them) that take up the same amount of time normally taken up by *two* of those notes.

Let's see how this works in the example above. The time normally taken up by "two of those notes" (in this time signature) is one beat, because the notes in question are eighth notes. Therefore, the three equal notes of the triplet also take up that much time—one beat!

Why do triplets cause difficulties for would-be sight-readers? A sight-reader who counts notes instead of beats surely has a difficult time trying to keep track of notes that last a third of a beat when his mind is settled into a meter in which the beat naturally divides itself into halves. Some sight-readers resort to the ineffective gimmick of mentally saying the words "one trip-let" or "tri-pl-et" whenever they see a triplet.

But, because you think in terms of beats, you have a better way of sight-reading triplets. You see the figure ♪♪♪ as something that takes up *one beat*. And what's the sound of that one beat? Why, you already know it, because back in Chapter 3 you memorized the sound of three equal attacks in a beat!

Exercises:

A. Playing Eighth Note Triplets

In this chapter, you don't need to memorize any new sounds. Instead, you'll learn to recognize alternate notations for sounds you already know. Note: Some sight-readers have a tendency to play ♪♪♪ when they see ♪♪♪. Make sure you play three *equal* attacks when playing triplets.

Discussion: Uneven Eighth Note Triplets

What about some of the other sounds you learned and memorized when studying compound time? How might they be notated in 2/4 time (or in any simple meter whose time signature has the bottom number "4")? Any quarter note beat can be shown to be divided into three equal parts (instead of the normal two) by writing the equivalent of three eighth notes with the numeral "3" above them. For example, the figure $\sqrt{}$ ♩ ♪ in 2/4 time sounds the same as the figure ♩ ♪ in 6/8 time (each lasts for one beat and each has attacks on the first and third parts of a fast "one-two-three").

For the purpose of further illustration, the chart below shows how some of the common one-beat figures you tapped in compound time are notated in 2/4 time (or in any simple meter whose time signature has the bottom number "4").

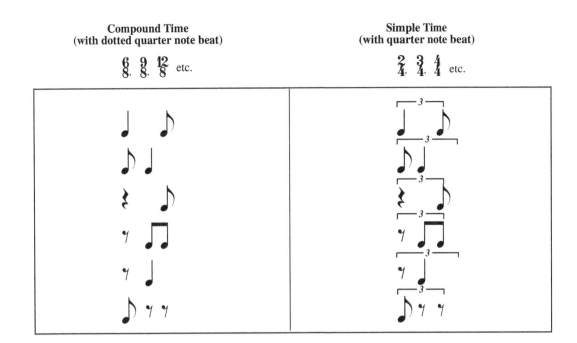

Exercises:

B. Playing Uneven Eighth Note Triplets

Tap the following:

Discussion: Quarter Note Triplets

In a simple meter whose time signature has the bottom number "2" (2/2, 3/2, etc.), three equal attacks are indicated not by an eighth note triplet, but by a *quarter note triplet* ($\overset{3}{\sqcap}$ ♩ ♩ ♩). This figure, of course, takes up the same amount of time normally taken up by two quarter notes—one beat!

Exercise:

C. Playing Quarter Note Triplets

Tap the following:

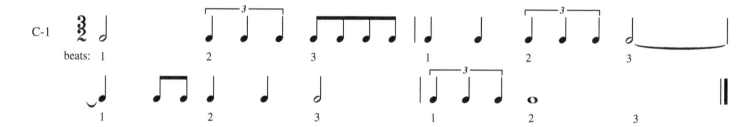

Discussion: Uneven Quarter Note Triplets

The other sounds you learned while studying compound time can also be indicated in a simple meter whose time signature has the bottom number "2." Any *half note* beat can be shown to be divided into three equal parts (instead of the normal two) by writing the equivalent of three *quarter notes* with the numeral "3" above them. For the purpose of illustration, the chart below shows how some of the common one-beat figures you tapped in compound time are notated in 2/2 time (or in any simple meter whose time signature has the bottom number "2").

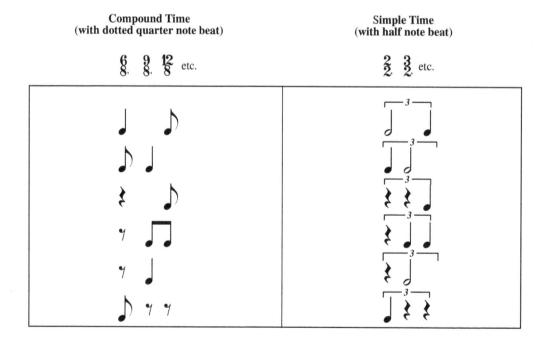

Exercises:

D. Playing Uneven Quarter Note Triplets

Tap the following:

Discussion: Two-Beat Triplets

In the examples above, the quarter note triplet took up one beat. But in 4/4 time (or in any simple meter whose time signature has the bottom number "4"), the quarter note triplet takes up *two* beats (because it takes up the time normally occupied by two quarter notes). Here we run into a potential complication: How should we tap a figure that takes up *two* beats if we've only learned those sounds that occur in *one* beat? Do we stop thinking in terms of beats and start thinking in terms of "two beats"? The answer is that you can still think in terms of beats if you realize that this figure: ♩ ♩ ♩ is identical to this one: ♩ ♪♪ ♩ (each has three equal attacks in two beats). And in the latter figure, you can recognize two familiar one-beat sounds, each of which is a type of eighth note triplet. The equivalency of the two figures and the dividing of the quarter note triplet into two separate one-beat sounds is demonstrated in the chart below.

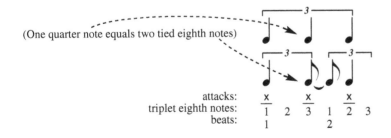

Exercise:

E. Playing Two-Beat Triplets

Tap the following:

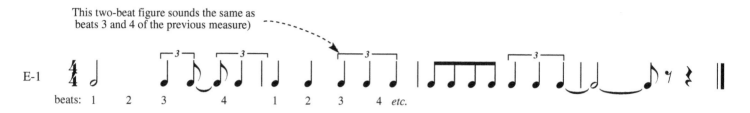

Discussion: Uneven Two-Beat Triplets

If we wish to divide two quarter note beats into three equal parts but to indicate attacks on only one or two of those parts, we modify the quarter note triplet by substituting a quarter rest for a quarter note (♩, for example) or by writing a half note in place of two quarter notes (♩, for example). But even these modified quarter note triplets can be sight-read fluently if you realize that each is identical in sound to a combination of two eighth note triplets (one beat each) whose sounds you already know. The chart below shows how each of the common modified quarter note triplets can be thought of as two one-beat sounds.

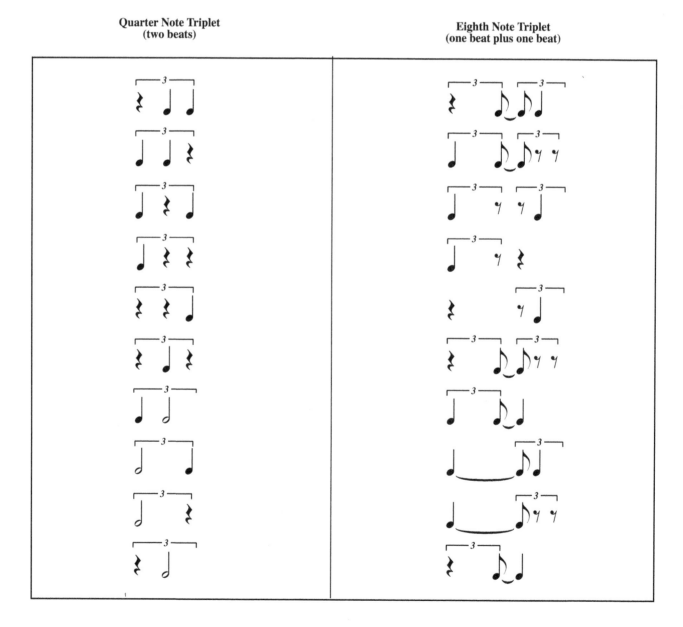

It might occur to you to ask why a notator would write the same figure sometimes as a quarter note triplet and sometimes as two eighth note triplets. In general, he chooses the notation that would be most easily read and understood. But if there's a second rhythm being played simultaneously (as in piano music or any music consisting of two or more parts), that second rhythm can help determine the notation of the first figure. The two examples below have the same right-hand rhythm, but in each case, the right-hand notation was determined by the rhythm of the left hand.

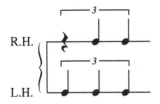 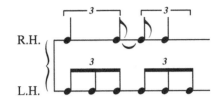

Exercise:

F. Playing Uneven Two-Beat Triplets

Tap the following:

Discussion: Duplets

In compound time, the beat naturally divides itself into three equal parts. But in spite of that natural subdivision, a composer writing in, say, 6/8 time might wish to indicate two equal attacks in one beat. How can he indicate this when these figures: ♪♩♪ and ♩.♩. (both of which indeed indicate two equal attacks in one beat) are awkward to read? The solution is to write a *duplet* (♩ ♩), in this case a *quarter note duplet*. What's a duplet? It's a group of two equal notes (with the numeral "2" placed above them) that take up the same amount of time normally occupied by three of the next smaller note value. The quarter note duplet (♩ ♩), for example, takes up the same amount of time as three eighth notes (one beat in 6/8 time).

Note: Some notators prefer to write a one-beat duplet in 6/8 (or similar time signatures) as two *eighth* notes (with the numeral "2" over them). But here we'll write these duplets as *quarters*, following the general rule that if you were to remove a "tuplet" numeral, you'd be left with "too much" music (as when, for example, if you were to remove the "3" from an eighth note triplet, your measure would contain an extra eighth note).

Exercises:

G. Playing Duplets

You already know the sound of two equal attacks in one beat. In the following examples, you need only learn to recognize an alternate notation for that sound.

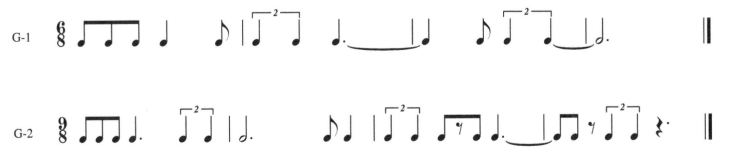

If we wish to divide a dotted quarter note beat into two equal parts, but to indicate an attack on only *one* of those parts, we modify the quarter note duplet by substituting a quarter rest for a quarter note . Of course, you're already familiar with the sounds of these two figures. In Chapter 2 we labeled the former sound "U" (attack on the upbeat only) and the latter sound "D" (attack on the downbeat only).

Another way to divide a dotted quarter note beat into two equal parts, but to indicate an attack on the upbeat only, is to write a quarter note duplet with a tie to the first note ().

Discussion: Quadruplets

We also might wish to indicate *four* equal attacks in one beat in compound time. This is accomplished by writing a *quadruplet*, which is a group of four equal notes (with the numeral "4" placed above them) that take up the time normally occupied by three of those notes. In 6/8 time (or in any compound meter whose time signature has the bottom number "8"), where one beat normally consists of three eighth notes, we write an *eighth note quadruplet* ( ) to indicate four equal attacks in one beat. And what's the sound of four equal attacks in one beat? Of course, it's the same sound you learned in Chapter 4 when you divided one beat in simple time into four equal parts (in a meter whose time signature has the bottom number "4," and in a meter whose time signature has the bottom number "2").

Exercises:

H. Playing Quadruplets

In the following examples, then, you don't need to learn a new sound—you need only recognize an alternate notation for an old one.

Discussion: Uneven Quadruplets

If we wish to divide one dotted quarter note beat into four equal parts, but to indicate attacks on only some of those parts, then we modify the eighth note quadruplet by: (1) substituting eighth rests for eighth notes (♩ or ♪, for example), (2) using a tie (♪♪♪), or (3) substituting one larger note for several smaller ones (♪♪♩ or ♩. ♪, for example). The various resultant sounds correspond to the sounds you learned in Chapter 4. For example, the figure ♩♪♪ in 6/8 time sounds the same as the figure ♩♪♪ in 2/4 time (in each, the beat is divded into four equal parts with attacks on the second, third, and fourth parts).

Exercises:

I. Playing Uneven Quadruplets

Again, in the following examples, you don't need to learn any new sounds—you need only recognize alternate notations for sounds you already know.

Note: Ex. I-2 contains so many beats that are divided into four parts instead of the normal three, that it could just as easily have been notated in simple time, as below. Tap the following:

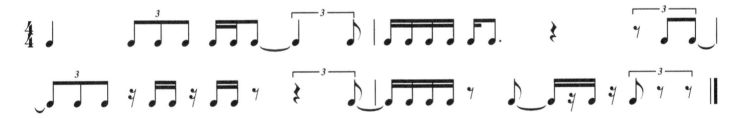

Discussion: A Matter of the Notator's Convenience

Is there any difference between the two examples above? Since the actual division of the beat alternates so often between one of four parts and one of three parts, the implied, natural subdivision of the beat is ambiguous. Therefore, the two examples are virtually the same. The choice of notation becomes a matter of the notator's convenience.

CHAPTER 6: FURTHER COMPLICATIONS

In this chapter you'll learn to recognize more alternate notations for familiar sounds. You'll also be confronted by some new, more complex sounds—ones you probably won't memorize—and you'll be given hints on how to deal with them (without having to resort to a pocket calculator).

Exercises:

A. The Eighth Note and the Whole Note Get the Beat

In Chapters 1 and 2, you tapped a total of only four different sounds. Those sounds were notated with a quarter note beat (in meters such as 4/4) or a half note beat (in meters such as 2/2). Those same sounds might also be notated with an *eighth* note beat.

And those same sounds might also be notated with a *whole* note beat.

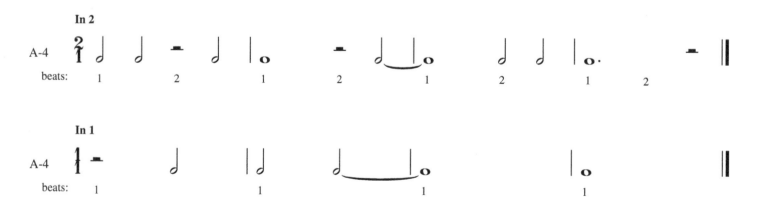

B. The Dotted Eighth Note Gets the Beat

In Chapter 3, where you studied compound time, you tapped a total of eight different sounds. These sounds were notated with a dotted quarter note beat (in meters such as 6/8) or a dotted half note beat (in meters such as 6/4). Those same sounds might also be notated with a dotted *eighth* note beat. In Chapter 3 you learned that we write 6/8 when we really intend 2/♩.. Likewise, we write 6/16 when we intend 2/♪..

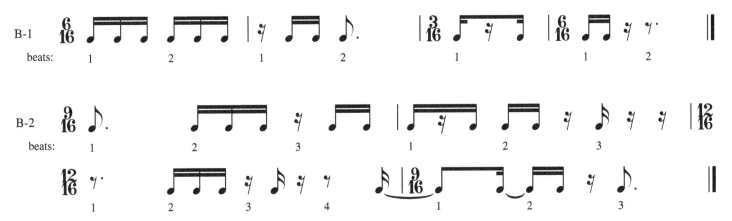

Discussion: New Sounds in Compound Time

When writing in compound time, composers sometimes indicate sounds other than the eight you memorized in Chapter 3. You might see an indication that one of the three eighth notes that make up a dotted quarter note beat is itself to be divided into two equal parts ♫♩♫, for example). Or maybe more than one of the eighth notes that make up the beat are to be subdivided ♫♪♫♫, for example).

How can you work out these complex sounds without actually dividing the beat into six tiny parts? Let's take the last sound mentioned (♫♪♫♫) as an example. First think of each eighth note as a separate beat, like this:

Or, if you find it easier, you can double all the values and think of three quarter note beats, like this:

Now you have three separate beats whose sounds you already know. If you can play those three sounds but *feel* them as one large beat instead of three small ones, you've succeeded in working out the complex, one-beat sound.

Exercises:

C. Playing New Sounds in Compound Time

In each of the examples below, work out the new sounds, then tap. (Don't try to memorize these new sounds.)

These same sounds might be notated in a compound meter whose time signature has the bottom number "4" with the dotted half note receiving the beat.

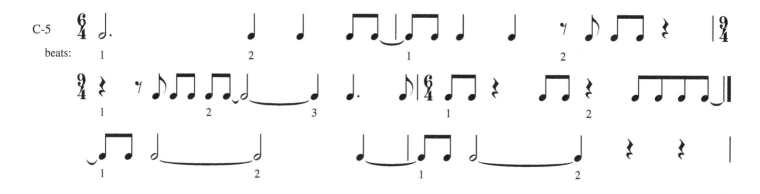

D. Playing in 2/1 and 1/1 Time

In Chapter 4, where the beat was divided into four equal parts, you tapped 16 different sounds. Those sounds were notated with a quarter note beat (in meters such as 4/4) or a half note beat (in meters such as 2/2). These same sounds might also be notated with a *whole* note beat.

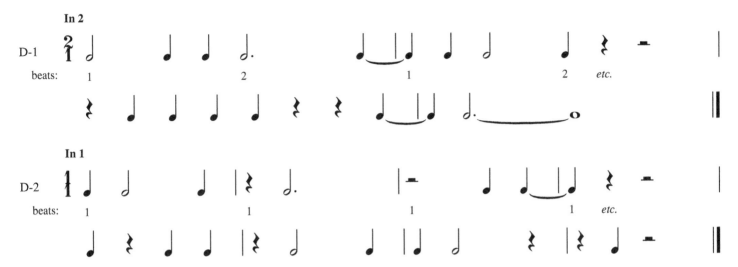

Discussion: New Sounds in Simple Time

Composers writing in simple time sometimes indicate sounds other than the 16 you memorized in Chapter 4. For example, you might see an indication that one of the four sixteenth notes that make up a quarter note beat is itself to be divided into two equal parts. In the figure ♫♫♫, for example, the fourth sixteenth note is divided into two *thirty-second notes* (a thirty-second note, indicated by three beams, is equal in duration to half a sixteenth note). Perhaps more than one sixteenth note is to be so divided (♫♫♫♫ or ♫♫♫♫♫, for example).

How can you work out these complex sounds without actually dividing the beat into a ridiculously large number of parts? Let's take this figure as an example: ♫♫♫♫. Again, you can first think of each eighth note as a separate beat. It's probably easier if you double all of the values and think of two quarter note beats, like this:

Now you have two separate beats whose sounds you already know. Again, if you can play those two sounds but *feel* them as one large beat instead of two small ones, you've worked out the one-beat sound.

Exercises:

E. Playing New Sounds in Simple Time

As before, work out the new sounds in each of the examples below, then tap. (Don't try to memorize these new sounds.)

Note: A *thirty-second rest* ( ) is equal in duration to a thirty-second note.

Those same sounds might also be notated in a simple meter whose time signature has the bottom number "2" (the *half* note receives the beat).

F. Playing One-Beat Triplets When the Eighth Note or Whole Note Gets the Beat

In Chapter 5 you learned that in simple time a triplet is used to indicate three equal attacks in one beat. The type of triplet you tapped (eighth note triplet, quarter note triplet, etc.) depended on the type of note receiving the beat, which in turn depended on the time signature. For example, in 4/4 time, where the quarter note receives the beat, you tapped an eighth note triplet (♪♪♪), and in 2/2 time, where the half note receives the beat, you tapped a quarter note triplet (♩♩♩).

In the example below, the *eighth* note receives the beat. Its division into three equal parts must be indicated by a *sixteenth* note triplet (♪♪♪), which is equivalent in duration to two sixteenth notes (or one eighth note).

When the *whole* note receives the beat, its division into three equal parts must be indicated by a *half* note triplet (♩♩♩), which is equivalent to two half notes (or one whole note).

Discussion: Two-Beat Triplets When the Half Note Gets the Beat

In the previous chapter, you learned that a triplet that takes up two beats (♩♩♩) can be thought of as two one-beat triplets (♩♪♪). Two-beat triplets can also be written in meters other than those whose time signatures have the bottom number "4."

In the example below, the half note receives the beat. The division of two beats into three equal parts must be indicated by a half note triplet (♩♩♩), which can be thought of as two one-beat triplets, like this: (♩♪♪♪).

Exercises:

G. Playing Two-Beat Triplets When the Half Note Gets the Beat
Tap the following:

H. Triplets That Take Up Half a Beat

Triplets can be used to indicate the division of any undotted note into three equal parts. In the two examples below, notes that take up only half a beat are so divided. Work out the new sounds, then tap.

I. Triplets That Take Up a Third of a Beat

In the next two examples, which are in compound time, a note that takes up only a third of a beat is to be divided into three equal parts. Work out the new sounds, then tap.

J. Dividing the Individual Notes of a Triplet

Sometimes one of the three notes that make up a triplet is itself to be divided into two parts (♩♫♫ or ♩♫♩, for example), or even three parts (♩ ♫♫♩ or ♩ ♩ ♫♫, for example). In the following, work out the new sounds, then tap.

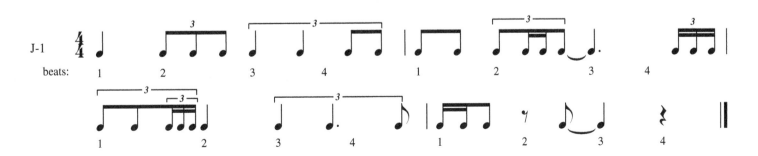

K. Duplets When the Dotted Half or Dotted Eighth Gets the Beat; Uneven Duplets

In the previous chapter, you learned that in compound time a duplet is used to indicate two equal attacks in one beat. You tapped quarter note duplets because the examples were written in meters in which the dotted quarter note received the beat.

In the example below, the dotted *half* note receives the beat. Its division into two equal parts must be indicated by a *half* note duple ( ).

In the next example, the dotted *eighth* note receives the beat. Its division into two equal parts must be indicated by an *eighth* note duplet ( ).

Sometimes one of the notes that make up the duplet is itself to be divided.

L. Quadruplets When the Dotted Half or Dotted Eighth Gets the Beat

In Chapter 5 you learned that in compound time a quadruplet is used to indicate four equal attacks in one beat. You tapped *eighth* note quadruplets because the examples were written in meters in which the dotted *quarter* note received the beat.

In the example below, the dotted *half* note receives the beat. Its division into four equal parts must be indicated by a *quarter* note quadruplet ( ).

In the next example, the dotted *eighth* note receives the beat. Its division into four equal parts must be indicated by a *sixteenth* note quadruplet ( ).

Discussion: Dividing Beats into Five, Six, Seven, or More Parts

Theoretically, any note, whether it receives the beat or not, can be shown to be divided into any number of equal parts. In the notation we've used so far, you've already seen several ways to indicate that a note is to be divided into two, three, or four equal parts. How might we indicate that a note is to be divided into five equal parts? Or six, or seven, or more?

We indicate a division into five equal parts by writing a *quintuplet*: a group of five equal notes (with the numeral "5" placed above them) that take up the time normally occupied by four of those notes. The quintuplet ♪♪♪♪♪, for example, is equal in duration to four sixteenth notes, or one quarter note. Likewise, we can show a division into six equal parts by writing a *sextuplet* (♪♪♪♪♪♪) and a division into seven equal parts by writing a *septuplet* (♪♪♪♪♪♪♪).

What about divisions into even *more* parts? The division of an undotted note into eight parts is, of course, shown without the use of an *octuplet* (eight equal notes with the numeral "8" placed above them), because for any undotted note, there exists a smaller note that's one-eighth its size. If, for example, we wish to indicate the division of a quarter note into eight equal parts, we simply write eight thirty-second notes (♪♪♪♪♪♪♪♪), because a thirty-second note equals an eighth of a quarter note. The indication of a division of a *dotted* note into eight equal parts, on the other hand, requires an octuplet.

How might we indicate that a note is to be divided into a great many equal parts? As an example, let's say that we want to show the division of a note into 13 equal parts. We write a figure that consists of one note for each of the 13 parts—13 notes. And above this figure we place the numeral that's the same as the number of notes in the figure—"13" (♪♪♪♪♪♪♪♪♪♪♪♪♪).

But we need a way of determining just how much time one of these complex figures takes up. Sometimes this can be determined simply by looking at the other notes in the measure and determining how much time they occupy; then we know how much time must be "left." For example, if a measure in 4/4 time consists of three quarter notes plus one crazily complicated figure, that figure must equal one quarter note. But when the situation isn't that clear, we still need a mathematical way of determining the total durations of these irregular figures.

Here's how it's done. Imagine that the numeral above the figure is removed. Now you're left with a figure that's actually too large. This becomes apparent when you recall that an eighth note triplet (♪♪♪) is equivalent to a quarter note. Without the numeral *3*, the remaining figure (♪♪♪) is larger than a quarter note. Now, imagine removing from the figure one note at a time until you have remaining the largest number of those notes that could normally be included with no numeral above them. If the figure is replacing an *undotted* note, that "largest number" would have to be one of the numbers in the series 2, 4, 8, 16, 32, etc., because these are the numbers of parts into which undotted notes can be shown to be divided without using a numeral. If, on the other hand, the figure is replacing a *dotted* note, that "largest number" would have to be one of the numbers in the series 3, 6, 12, 24, etc., because these are the numbers of parts into which dotted notes can be shown to be divided without using a numeral.

So, going back to our example of one note divided into thirteen equal parts, we can determine that if the figure is replacing an undotted note, the figure (with three beams in this case) must be equivalent to a quarter note.

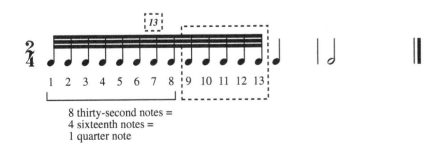

8 thirty-second notes =
4 sixteenth notes =
1 quarter note

If the figure is replacing a dotted note, the figure must be equivalent to a dotted quarter note.

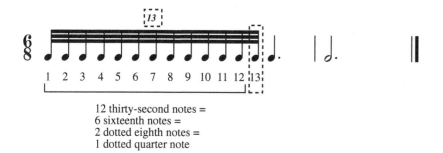

12 thirty-second notes =
6 sixteenth notes =
2 dotted eighth notes =
1 dotted quarter note

Exercises:

M. Playing Beats Divided into Many Parts

In the following examples, work out the new sounds, then tap.

M-1

The sextuplet has a special problem, because when a note is divided into six equal parts, there might be some question concerning the relative stresses of the six notes. If we divide a quarter note, for example, into six equal parts, do we tap like this:

(1) ; like this:

(2) ; or like this:

(3) ?

To avoid possible confusion, notators usually write the first figure above like this: and the second figure above like this: .

M-2

Discussion: The Note Receiving the Beat Changes: Counting Notes Instead of Beats

Throughout this book you've been told to count beats, not notes, because counting notes can only lead to defeat. But in one rhythmic situation, the only way to sight-read successfully is to do the very thing you've been warned not do to—count notes! The situation I'm referring to is one in which, due to a temporary meter change, the beat—which you'd been contentedly counting—ceases to exist. In measure 3 of the example below, for example, you must stop counting beats and actually count eighth notes.

Exercises:

N. Playing by Counting Notes Instead of Beats

Tap the following:

The equivalency (♪ = ♪) placed above the 5/8 shows that the eighth note of the 4/4 measures is equal in duration to the eighth note in the 5/8 measure.

Here are some more examples:

Even though there are some rhythms out there in the world that are even more complex and scary than any we've covered in this book, you should now have all the tools you need to handle just about any normal sight-reading situation. So get out there and sight-read; and remember—*count beats!*

Appendix A: Glossary

Bar line

Beats are often felt in groups of two, three, or four. After each group of beats, we draw a vertical line called a *bar line* (|). At the end of a composition, we draw a thin bar line followed by a thick bar line (‖).

Measure

The space between two consecutive bar lines is called a *measure* or a *bar*.

Time signature

Two numbers, one placed above the other, appear at the beginning of a composition. These numbers are called a *time signature*.

The bottom number is especially important because it tells us something that can't be learned in any other way: which kind of note (eighth note, quarter note, half note, etc .) is to receive one beat. How does it tell us? The bottom number is thought of as the denominator of a fraction whose numerator is 1. A bottom number of "4," for instance, tells us that the quarter note (♩) should receive one beat. Similarly, a bottom number of "2" tells us that the half note (♩) should receive one beat, and a bottom number of "8" tells us that the eighth note (♪) should receive one beat.

The top number tells us *how many beats* should occur in each measure. (This information can also be obtained by examining the music and simply counting the number of beats in each measure.)

Meter

Meter, which is dictated by the time signature, refers to the number of beats in a measure, the relative stresses (weak or strong) of those beats, and the natural division into parts (two or three) of each beat.

1 whole note =

2 half notes =

4 quarter notes =

8 eighth notes =

16 sixteenth notes =

32 thirty-second notes =

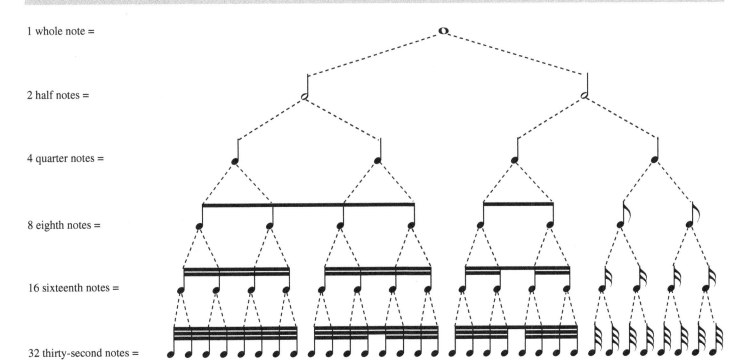

More Great Piano/Vocal Books

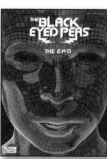

FROM CHERRY LANE

For a complete listing of Cherry Lane titles available,
including contents listings, please visit our web site at
www.cherrylane.com